9×11

Other books by Michael Turner

Company Town
Hard Core Logo
Kingsway
American Whiskey Bar
The Pornographer's Poem
8×10

9 × 11

and other poems like Bird, Nine, x, and Eleven

Michael Turner

New Star Books | Vancouver | 2018

NEW STAR BOOKS LTD.

107 – 3477 Commercial Street, Vancouver, BC V5N 4E8   CANADA

1574 Gulf Road, No. 1517, Point Roberts, WA 98281   USA

www.NewStarBooks.com   info@NewStarBooks.com

The publisher acknowledges the financial support of the Canada Council
for the Arts and the British Columbia Arts Council.

Cataloguing information for this book is available from Library and
Archives Canada, www.collectionscanada.gc.ca.

Book design by Robin Mitchell Cranfield

Printed and bound in Canada by Imprimerie Gauvin, Gatineau, QC

First published September 2018

"*All the terrible tragedy of life would be attributable to our dislocation in time and space; but since time and space are merely our way of perceiving things, but otherwise have no reality, even the greatest tragic pain must be explicable to those who are truly clear-sighted as no more than the error of the individual.*"

Letter from Wagner to Mathilde Wesendonck,
dated August 1860

For Stan Douglas

9×11

A small room behind a bay window. A single bed, a table and chair, and a sink. I could manage something larger, with more conveniences, but I could never match the view.

Inside the glassed-in porch hang seven mailboxes, one for each room in the house. If I have not picked up my mail by ten-thirty, the tenant in 7 slips it under my door.

This morning I awoke to something skidding towards me. I could almost reach it, but when I saw what it was, I rolled over. A clear blue sky. In the corner of the window, a jet.

II

The aerograms have been arriving once a month for a year. The news is never good. The sender is well and lists her activities with a lash. It is the lash I read, not the writing.

The opening paragraph could be Auster. You can see the care taken. After that, point-form declarations. The whip pulled back. The exclamation mark at the end — is me!

I drift off. When I open my eyes, the plane is gone. Only its vapour trail remains: parallel lines followed by fraying, dissipation. I roll over and reach for the aerogram.

III

There are four rooms on the top floor: the northeast corner (4), the southeast corner (5) and the northwest corner (7). I live between the southwest corner and the southeast corner, in 6.

At the southwest corner is a bathroom. Between it and the northwest corner is a toilet. Running east to west is a hallway that opens north halfway, where it meets the stairs — six to the landing, twelve more to the door.

I took this room five years ago, as an office. I was having trouble concentrating and thought a dedicated space would provide focus. I have never been so productive.

IV

The tenant in 5 has lived here the longest. She insists we live by her rules. After bathing we are to scrub the tub until it squeaks. The first time I did this I worked so hard I had to bathe again.

Same goes for the toilet. The tenant in 5 does not like aerosols and insists we use a candle, even though the room is barely big enough for one person, let alone one plus an open flame.

The tenant in 4 is heavyset and has long hair. After moving in she lit the candle on the water tank and sat down to do her business. A crackle, followed by intense heat. You could smell her hair for a week.

V

The tenant in 4 has been here second-longest. Like me, she took the room as a workplace. What that work is, I do not know. When we bump into each other she speaks of it so abstractly it could be anything.

"I have so much work on my plate," she says wearily, and I nod gravely. Then she looks me in the eye, like I might want to know, but no, I prefer not to.

There are some things worth knowing and some things I can live without. Some things keep me guessing, and I enjoy the exercise. The rest is conditioning — stock narratives, stereotypes, anything received.

VI

This month's aerogram has its sender in Yemen. As usual, the letter begins with a well-written description of her surroundings, then those lashes.

She is working for an NGO, but she does not say which one. Nor can I infer. Much of the content is related to meals. You would think she is working for *Zagat*.

Unlike her previous aerograms, this one has a conclusion, a poorly-written paragraph about avoiding tall buildings. From restaurant dishes to plate tectonics, this woman is an expert on everything.

VII

We have been notified that our rent is going up. I am currently paying $396 a month, what I paid when I moved in. Next month it will be $415.80, an increase of five percent.

When I took the place I was curious about the figure, how it was arrived at, why it was not rounded off. I thought it might be related to the square footage of the room, so I measured it.

The east and west walls are nine feet long, the north and south walls eleven. Nine times eleven is ninety-nine, ninety-nine times four is what I once paid in rent.

VIII

The ladybird by my foot occupies less than a square inch of floor space. I think of myself in relation to this room. If an inch was a foot, I would have 14,256 square feet to work with.

The trading floor of the New York Stock Exchange is to feet what my room is to inches. The ladybird seems to know this, her eyes scanning the board, waiting for her price. Is she buying, selling? Waiting, waiting…

So patient, this ladybird. I want her to lift off, make that noise, prove my imagination correct. What is she waiting for? Does she know? Is there anything I can do? Shoo, ladybird! Shoo!

IX

The tenant in 7 has his TV turned up. He does this when there is
breaking news. I stumble from my bed and head for the bath. His door is
open, he wants company. There are some things worth knowing

and some things I can live without. Like the tenant in 7. He moved in a
week before me and treats me like I am on probation, slipping me notes
about loud music, which I never play, coming home late and waking him.

The bathtub is a claw-foot, super deep. I crawl inside before turning on
the taps and wait for the water to lift me. Once he slipped me a note for
staying in too long, even though he bathes in the evening.

X

My current project is based on the later poems of Baudelaire. I have on my table a copy of *Paris Spleen* and a stack of books about his work, stuff that is not yet online.

I am interested in his thoughts on poetry, how he arrived at making poetry through prose. I am less interested in distinguishing between poetry and prose than I am in our perceptions of them.

Perceptions are what I am particularly interested in, like what I said about stock narratives, stereotypes... Perceptions, like nightingales, are two things poets have to work with.

XI

For the past hour I have sat in my dressing gown watching TV at 7's. Commentators keep saying how the world will never be the same. All of them have U.S. accents.

I am on my second cup of tea when, for the umpteenth time, 7 echoes their sentiments. Until then, I knew little about him, but now I know he was a soldier

and that he likes to keep his "finger in," as he puts it. I have also learned that he knows things about me he could only know from reading my mail. Behind him, almost hidden by a book, lies an opened stack of aerograms.

the morning air does not part it pushes and in pushing sticks to my face

making this face the face I look for in the first window I pass the vain face the face that looks for itself and in looking finds not what it looks like but

a record of what motivates the looking is what I have learned from looking across the street a car its driver smiling waving me over in his other hand a map shrugging his grin says he has given up and I find it exhilarating that a man with a map could be that happy at not arriving it is so rare

these days to meet such a man I feel my face change just thinking about it

21

rushing to him like a lover he sees in my face this change I can tell because

it is no longer what he cannot find that has him waving but where we are now at exactly this moment and what came before it is something we know

and that is the news we awoke to and stayed in our undies for hours to watch its billowing images but worse the descriptions of what we could clearly see

for ourselves the nervous speculations over who could have done such a thing and what consequences would that have on what is sure to follow and how would that affect subsequent programming and we agreed that this was what kept us wondering when would they run the first advertisement and

what would that ad be whether the decision to not run ads would come from the advertisers or the networks because who makes these decisions

and why was this not discussed in concert with what we were watching because someone has to pay for these talking heads these camera operators those who answer the phones and guard the doors this conversation between the producers and the advertisers like the car honking and me

running to it indeed the first paid ad should be remembered as the moment

this country stepped from its mirror sniffed at its humility and announced
to the world that its convalescence is over

Directions

East to the end of the block, then south two more are my directions,
how I arrive at coffee after climbing out of bed, washing up, the
bowl of cereal eaten with rice milk and berries. What makes these
blocks more than breadcrumbs are the houses I pass, reminders
that we live in History.

Edwardian houses like the one I depart from; Craftsman bungalows
from the thirties and forties; tiny "war" houses built for returning
servicemen; "Vancouver Specials", whose labour-saving design
is based on the factory-produced 4×8-foot sheet of plywood;
"monster" houses associated with eighties immigration;

and this new one I keep seeing, a hybrid whose exterior is happily
romantic, but whose interior is rational, modern, geared at efficient
living: getting the children to school; their parents to work; then
eight hours later, the reverse.

A crowd gathers outside the house across the street: a recently
refurbished church manse and a coach house that was once its
garage. They await the arrival of the most important person in their
lives right now — the realtor who will tour them through this strata-
title village.

A "garden level" two-bedroom listed at a half-a-million and a three
bedroom above it for twice that. The coach house is "just under a
million," "just low enough to excite an auction," as if buying a house
is no longer putting in an offer and waiting, but screaming from the
stock exchange floor.

31

I make my way down the steps as a middle-aged man breaks from the crowd. He canters towards me, his daughter on his shoulders, her neck snapping back. "You live here?" he demands, and I struggle with the question. Not what it wants, but where it is headed, what the years have taught me.

Two Cafés

The café is run by a French couple from Grenoble. They start work at 5 a.m., bake their own goods and serve coffee roasted at a warehouse in Burnaby.

On this morning I bump into Zbigniew. He is walking his dog, an older-than-he-looks golden retriever named Tyson. Because both of us are walking in the same direction, we do not stop. The café is CLOSED FOR THE HOLIDAYS.

Like Tyson, Zbigniew looks older than he is. Same with Marina, his wife. Both Zbigniew and Marina emigrated from Poland after Marina gave birth to their eldest, who, at fifteen, now towers over his parents and could pass for their grandson.

Zbigniew asks where I have coffee when the café I closed. I tell him the café two blocks east. He knows the one. Like me, he goes there when he has to. He says, "There is a sadness to owner," and I concur. But sadness is not a word I would use.

The owner is also from Europe, though I am not sure where. The first time he served me was three years ago, a sunny day between Christmas and New Year's. He stood too close, spoke too loud. I could understand if he was Latin, but he is not. He is not Latin.

Breath

"In the clouds," he begins, his breath heavy on the "s", as if it
was hissing from the tire of the car across the street – FOR SALE:
$1100.

"Do you know the origin of the dollar sign?" he asks, and because
there are many I say, "Yes, there are many," and he begins again:

"Baudelaire's stranger loved clouds. Not family or friends, not
country or beauty or gold, but clouds" — and again with the "s",
only louder.

I close my laptop, get up to leave, when he grabs my arm and
says it again.

Synesthesia

coffee is no longer where it comes from but how
when the means are increasingly assumed
ethics you can taste, politics on the tip of your tongue
the roof of the mouth is still a roof like ketchup is a vegetable
food and shelter — the irreducible minimum — and from this seed
a stadium, the welfare state, with its own lip service paid for by
Postwar Economic Growth, the team that keeps on winning
the United States the Globetrotters, the Generals everyone else
not a cosmos but a line ascending, the straighter the better
like those Apollo rockets and their ferocious lift-offs
not The Economy we were watching but a rehearsal
of that which has become a tendency to associate rockets
with economies, not the opposite of bombs dropped
concurrently on Hanoi, Nam Dinh and Viet Tri
but the appearance of an opposite
because what was sent to the moon
and what fell on North Vietnam
was the coffee mom bought at the supermarket
the loss-leader bananas that lured her there
coffee still comes from the same places
but it is the treatment of its pickers
that gives it its taste

U.S. Birth Graph*

behind a decommissioned half-track

on the kitchen table, the radio blaring

in the middle of a raspberry u-pick

while waiting at a railway crossing

ten minutes into a twenty-minute nap

inspired by a new and improved design

at a time of global economic certainty

with no thought given to the neighbours

despite recent gains in public awareness

beside the window, the television blaring

*the characters that appear on each line and
the spaces between the words they form
represent 100,000 "live" births in the United
States between 1946–1964

under the influence of Lysol Disinfectant

between a glass of wine and a box of novels

eight days before the next menstrual cycle

immediately following the six o'clock news

against all odds — and a lattice-work fence

where demand for reconciliation appears low

towards the Advancement of Colored People

below a yellowing photo of John Bell Hood

beyond what passes for stasis and change

Skyscrapers

Only in its shape did the poem anticipate the skyscraper. Rising up as History, a firm unyielding finger. Sssh! it says — *I am all ye need to know.* Each floor just wide enough to support the next; each line similarly measured, in feet, with space on either side.

Tickertape and cash register receipts carry their facts on paper just wide enough to support them, its ink just dark enough. Who would expect more from that which is concerned only with proof of our transactions, that which is bought and sold? The tickertape machine and the cash register are U.S. inventions; both were introduced in the years that followed the American Civil War.

At the end of the nineteenth century, after the appearance of the first skyscrapers, Mallarmé published "Un coup de dés n'abolira le hasard" in *Cosmopolis*. There is no correlation between the skyscraper and Mallarmé's poem, but let us consider them together: the skyscraper mimics the poem as we knew it, while Mallarmé's poem abandons the vertical structure for what was once the poem's margins, filling them with birdsong, confetti, or more recently, bodies from a burning tower.

Years earlier, in *Paris Spleen*, Baudelaire asks Arsène Houssaye:

"Which one of us, in his moments of ambition, has not dreamed of the miracle of a poetic prose, musical, without rhythm and without rhyme, supple enough and rugged enough to adapt itself to the lyrical impulses of the soul, the undulations of reverie, the jibes of consciousness?"

Baudelaire arrived at this question "out of [his] exploration of huge cities, out of the medley of their innumerable interrelations," and he did so in advance of the skyscrapers that now define them. As for ticker tape, it was not their machines that gave us the first ticker tape parade but the skyscraper. The first ticker tape parade came with the dedication of France's gift to the United States — the Statue of Liberty. Without those skyscrapers, from where might this tape have fallen?

Bird

for Judy Radul

I did not know enough about you yet

apart from your presence that day

not a crow or a robin or a sparrow

but something unsettled deep in a tree

staring back at me was the song I gave you

my way of saying that what I was seeing was real

that you were here for a reason

to teach me that I was real

and you were a bird

Nine

I know how old I was but it is the year I keep thinking of
the last Sunday in August barely my age the tracks
curving east through a heat ripple a portal
impossible to enter we agreed
or exit someone added

it had not occurred to us
someone's cousin a visitor to our world
as if our world was something to step into
was how I heard it
too young to say such a thing
younger than I was in '71

X

no mark so anonymous as to obscure what lies behind it

in science the symbol x is a variable an *unknown value to find*

while its capitalization hidden behind my shift function

was chosen by the poet X. J. Kennedy to obscure his second name

whose initial he switched with his first to distinguish himself

from Boston's Joseph P. Kennedy

unlike the "S" in Harry S. Truman who became president

where Joseph P. failed the "S" standing not for variability

the names of Truman's maternal and paternal grandfathers

but what mattered most to Joseph P. and that is patriarchy

Eleven

a time for which memories require internet assistance
who has not begun such a journey with a song
Billboard's spreadsheet streetscape the number one slot
a shop "The Morning After" next door to Diana Ross
pleading for someone to "Touch Me in the Morning"
of my birthday the Stories' interracial love affair
Marvin Gaye's contracted pronoun wafting over
the cannery's softly-rotting boardwalk
"Half-Breed" as I enter Grade Six "Angie"
among the washers in their bright white coveralls
smoking laughing marching from the plant

Cold War

all day long we accumulate, and when we stop to ask ourselves why
we are shown a Soviet bread line, or a winter's day in July

a spy satellite explodes — the Space Shuttle — and Israel responds
with bombs on Southern Lebanon

South Africa is a class problem, not a race problem, and for saying so
she is beaten by her sisters

all day long we accumulate, engage in some form of pyramid-making
while our elected officials sit around untelevised

peeling back the welfare state, removing what is conducive, tossing its
shielding aside

we knew it was wrong, we protested, but we never imagined what it
would look like, what monsters it might inspire

now they are here — not up top but among us, our friends suddenly
full of shrugs where once they had thoughts, comments

let the market decide is a friend of that shrug, and I want to kill myself
return to what was best about my youth and how it works in heaven

Untitled
for Amy Kazymerchyk

a walk alone not lonely
amidst ourselves as thought
as always

thoughts of others
theirs of us shadows past
lives fertilize what is about to

blossom an absence not
of space but of time for now
what is coming as always plans

made and kept a passing held
like blossoms gathered
a light left on this morning

goes undetected
yet at night returning
a window glows in waiting

Avanti's

for Deanna Ferguson

its draw was no distance
so I went don't belonging
for sip lifting cold off
touch dining from nut bowl
too hot August Sunday
a four o'clock wander
I could've gone further
if for loneliness wanting
but quaffing's belonging
like chit-chat's to tipping
the servers were telling
me nuts don't sell bottles
that snacks eat excuses
I was pinting to swelling

48

so followed the next day
the take up the same seat
a stare past the dart board
in five o'clock sunlight
I count on my money
to add up my drinking
four mugs to the hour
seemed average for spending
so passed on the next one
to swim by this server
a one from the Sunday
whose name like Maria
I waved from the exit
to no one was watching

a continue to Tuesday

the barman did nodding

I take up the same seat

near Maria seen waiting

the usual wording

my order her question

so even a yes please

was even less talking

the pops off the dart board

were two keeners tossing

their squawk about Expo

so workplace exotic

spilled out of the window

the grey sky to breaking

a new scene the Wednesday
the welfare cheques cashing
meant fresh staff and muscle
for the clientele party
I stuck out as something
that felt don't familiar
a slow motion touchdown
for nothing but silence
save hard rock and knee slaps
some boner gone boasting
I stretched myself sitting
then leaned back remanded
if push comes to walking
I'd rather play hockey

Thursday the seat saved
I'm thanked by Maria
the barman starts pumping
a thumbs up for something
the drink is a freebie
a not what I'm wanting
this premium whiskey
for promoting a bouncing
last night I was blocking
two guys off the porter
I'd almost forgotten
my boozing so sleepy
I go to bed walking
heads up in the foggy

Friday's a line up
a move to the front of
to don't see the panic
the furniture laughing
the doorman's important
he pulls me in quickly
my seat is vacated
and wiped away popcorn
it's always this busy
this time on a pay day
Maria says changing
her tip jar bouqueting
I can't see the dart board
the window pane heading

same day's the next day
the last call is ringing
a goodbye Maria
to wipes off my table
my name's not Maria
just everyone says so
the barman's get going
my no for an answer
I jump up so loaded
my spill off the floor show
a blindside so numbing
I watched as it happened
my body's don't going
they carried me throwing

Vial

what it comes in and when

what comes in it is finished

a tiny glass cylinder with

an end and an opening and a

tiny tiny cork that got lost in

its emptying stands small on

the window sill O'ing O O

O O mOre than just empty

is all O O O O that is left

O O O O O Of O O O O it

POtiOn

O O O O that Peruvian rag
the alpaca O O O who stOOd
fOr it O O beside O O the fire
birds O O O O up O O O up
O O the chimney O O cOpper
gOblets' O O O O bellies O O
O O O glOw O O taxidermy's
glass-eyed Owl O O O gOes
hOOOO-hOOO O O a blue
saucer O O O a crust Of pie

Genie

sO O O O O O Orange O O O
O O in O O O its O O O O O
furnace O O O O O smOke the
O O O genie O O O falls O O
O O O O O O O O O O O frOm
the O O O O ceiling O O O O O
O O O O O O O O O O legless
yOur O O O O O O O O O O O
O O O wish O O O O O O O O
O O O O O O O O O is O O O

57

O

O O O O O O O O O O O O O
O O O O O O O O O O O O O
O O O O O O O O O O O O O
O O O O O O O O O O O O O
O O O O O O O O O O O O O
O O O O O O O O O O O O O
O O O O O O O O O O O O O
O O O O O O O O O O O O O
O O O O O O O O O O O O O
O O O O O O O O O O O O O

Cork

like lose a verb but like its noun

found the vial once again corked

rolling between thumb forefinger

passed absently from hand to hand

where it is rolled again and again

the air trapped a thought had or

imagined a fact a fabrication to be

deployed saved but the cork is there

pressed into place designed neither

to fit nor protect only to remain

Passe-Partout

for Peter Culley

doctors all yourself

bounds not where

it hurts or when

a numbness does

its presence such

as stopped to light

dumb rustles felt

a feathered breath

since ferns from this

is listened into

pictures

watchers call on elves

hounds are there

this flirts for sense

the wonder of

its pheasant bunch

past all last night

some dozen welts

untethered hence

it burns from this

it glistens in you

sutured

poachers caught on film
soundless air
within this fence
an unspooled stump
this pleasant lunch
with all its might
no one to help
another went
pictures of him
en passe-partout
torture

climbing up an elm

on a dare

hitherto dead

what fooled you once

is too much fun

give up the sight

so much for self

a plundered sense

midges hover

in this instance

aborted

falling on post-health
bounds not where
this flirts for sense
an unspooled stump
is too much fun
as stopped to light
past all last night
with all its might
a feathered breath
it burns from this
en passe-partout

Wheelbarrow

the introduction of colour into the poem
is its reconsideration as design no longer
a skeleton we clothe but a wheelbarrow
whose adjective is redundant replaced
by *so much depends upon* printed in
the colour the adjective describes I try
this without writing it and the poem still
moves with the grace Williams gave it
the rain enhanced by a glossier finish
chickens whitest between each word

Design

with principles so rigid so immutable
you would think they were devised by
someone who had spent time in eyes
nowhere else do you see this insistence
on what can and cannot be done with
a line a margin are you sure you mean
that I am asked when a word falls onto
the following page a word orphaned with
all that space is not a waste because the
lines in this poem are one word long

Dance

I am only prepared to go so far — to here
the tip of my middle finger if I was to use
my arm but only to here and again you
try and again you take it too far so don't
when I use my arm look at me like that
when I am talking to you don't you know
how rude it is to not look at the person
talking to you look at where my arm is —
to here this time all the way out to here
look look look at where my arm is now

every word, every letter in every word, every word in every sentence, so perfectly placed, like this one

Fugue

for Janet Cardiff and George Bures Miller

Muse

The story is told of a woman who broke into the home of another woman, a writer, and forced her from her bed and into her study, where for the next three hours she held a gun to her head after whispering the words, "Now write."

"It is difficult to write under such conditions," the writer kept saying, writing, but at the end of three hours she happily announced that she might have the start of something, and that, said the intruder, was all she needed to hear.

Music

The story under consideration is that of pianist who, after years of working as an accompanist, playing whatever was put before him, begins a composition based on the number of keys in a piano.

The idea is that each piano key would be played no more than once, and that each key would have a word assigned to it, but that the word, which is to be sung, would carry a note different from the one assigned to the key.

The title of the composition is *Finished Business*.

Sickness

"It's a sad story," he said, lighting his pipe.

"Will you share it with me?" the arranger asked gently.

"Hell no!" he exhaled.

"Why not?" asked the arranger.

"'Why not? asked the arranger,'" she said to herself mockingly, replacing "his pipe" with "a cigarette."

Essence

It is not so much a story based on a change of fortune — the complexity, crisis and threat that occurs in advance of the story's climax and the resolution of the problem that completes it — but a condition independent of it.

This condition remains at the heart of her composer's character, regardless of what befalls him. For he is a melancholic, and no matter how hard he tries to rise above or sink below his condition, he is, like the book before her, bound by it.

Celebration

"I don't normally write stories that background our present condition," she says into the microphone, wishing she had said it differently, the room still echoing with shouts of bravo and applause.

Setting her speech aside, she begins again — this time tearfully. "You crave stories in the same way you crave a town after hours of highway driving, the eccentricity of its architecture, its people, when it is how similar these towns are to your own that you can't stop chewing on, that lulls us all to sleep!"

Surrey Intellectuals

who am I to know this writing for
a waves its blackened screech
palms at the heels as wings go
frozen in an instance of falling
to feed upon its ink

readings taken and made
pattern of consumption its own
mess the text suggests what's left
potential for additional subtractions
not the story of a bird but its form

a cold grey windowlessness
a condition an atmosphere
measures paced with fence posts
barbs notes to sing along with
the sun in love our bouncing ball

automotive hymn book shifts
a choir wakes to its refrain
who am I to know this singing for
if not to keep this bird afloat
my hands below the landscaped page

Say it with Diamonds

Prologue

what anger forms
this stone is shown

carved is art
but a jewel must be cut

who says it is
a shield before injury kneeling

sword in hand
a cross that cries by right

76

Table

gathered to face
the interior administration

of trustworthy light
equal until otherwise

a documentation problem
da Vinci's diners face out

a facet for each knight
does not always make it round

Crown

down and outwards
a susceptible angle

the collected scratches
a history of resistance

its rule and its injustices
gold's purple abdication

gone fishin' is free
to lure each shilling

Girdle

a border
not a cinch

to look at
catch light

its top assumes
a bottom

an indifferent gesture
sparkles at night

Pavilion

on climbing days
cutting feet

legs swinging
the body in each finger

under the weather
protected

with every ascent
a pulling

Culet

flat or pointed
goes unseen

a spinning top
is not about

what goes on
below

but what comes up
from under

Personal

Eurasian moment with chronic neo-liberal distention looking to
turn time into space. Of variable means, prone to malaise but never
lazy, and a heart — OMG! a heart that is large and getting larger!
If you are worldwide, sustainable, intentional and metaphysical,
could we meet again, start over?

Acknowledgments

The writing of this book was supported by a British Columbia Arts Council grant. Some of the poems appeared in the above/ground press chapbook series, *BOO, The Capilano Review, West Coast Line, Misfit Lit* (Kwantlen Polytechnic University), *This Now, More Than Ever* (SFU Gallery), and *websit*.

Biography

Michael Turner was born in North Vancouver, B.C. in 1962 and spent his teenage summers working in the Skeena River salmon fishery. After high school, he travelled through Europe and North Africa, eventually to the University of Victoria, where he completed a BA (anthropology) in 1986. Between 1987–1993 he sang and played banjo in Hard Rock Miners; upon his retirement from touring, he opened the Malcolm Lowry Room (1993–1997). His first book, *Company Town* (1991), was nominated for a Dorothy Livesay Poetry Prize. His second book, *Hard Core Logo*, was adapted to feature-film. *Kingsway* (1995), *American Whiskey Bar* (1997), *The Pornographer's Poem* (1999) and *8×10* (2009) followed. A frequent collaborator, he has written scripts with Stan Douglas, poems with Geoffrey Farmer and songs with cub, Dream Warriors, Fishbone and Kinnie Starr. He blogs at this address mtwebsit@blogspot.com.